RUBBER BAND SCIENCE

John Perritano

Created by Q2AMedia

www.q2amedia.com

Text, design & illustrations Copyright © Leopard Learning 2009

Editor Jessica Cohn
Editorial Director Bonnie Dobkin
Client Service Manager Santosh Vasudevan
Project Manager Shekhar Kapur
Art Director Sumit Charles
Designers Shilpi Sarkar, Parul Gambhir and Joita Das
Illustrators Ishan Varma, Sumeet Surve, Sachin Dadlani,
        Madhavi Poddar and Abhijeet Sharma
Art Editor Sreshtha Bhattacharya
Picture Researcher Anju Pathak

10 9 8 7 6 5 4 3 2 1

ISBN: 978-0-545-23971-4

Contents

Behold, the Rubber Band!

The ancient Maya used them to tie ax blades to wooden sticks.

Joel Waul of Lauderhill, Florida, wrapped more than 720,000 of them together, making a huge ball. It weighed 9,032 pounds (4,097 kilograms) when sent to a museum.

Bart Simpson used one big one to make a slingshot.

Welcome to the wonderful, stretchable world of rubber bands.

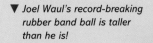

▼ *Joel Waul's record-breaking rubber band ball is taller than he is!*

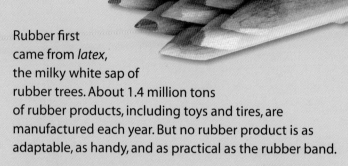

Rubber first came from *latex*, the milky white sap of rubber trees. About 1.4 million tons of rubber products, including toys and tires, are manufactured each year. But no rubber product is as adaptable, as handy, and as practical as the rubber band.

Major Dates in Rubber Band History

1839

Charles Goodyear accidentally discovers **vulcanization**, the process that makes rubber elastic.

▲ *Goodyear discovered vulcanization after five years of research.*

1845

Stephen Perry invents the modern rubber band.

1923

William Spencer, of Alliance, Ohio, cuts up rubber in his basement and starts the first rubber-band business.

Wacky Elastic

The U.S. Postal Service is the largest consumer of rubber bands in the United States.

It's a Stretch!

About 1,000 years ago, the Maya of Mexico and Central America created the first rubber bands. They took the sap from rubber trees, dried it over a fire, and created a stretchable strip.

Now, rubber bands come in all shapes, sizes, and colors. Some are made from natural rubber. Others are **synthetic**. Rubber bands have an amazing ability to stretch, twist, and change back into their original shape—a concept known as *elasticity*.

▲ Latex is a sap that comes from rubber trees.

Synthetic rubber is made from crude oil. The oil is trucked to factories.

The oil is mixed with a kind of soap in machines called *reactors*. The rubber that is created can be made into rubber products.

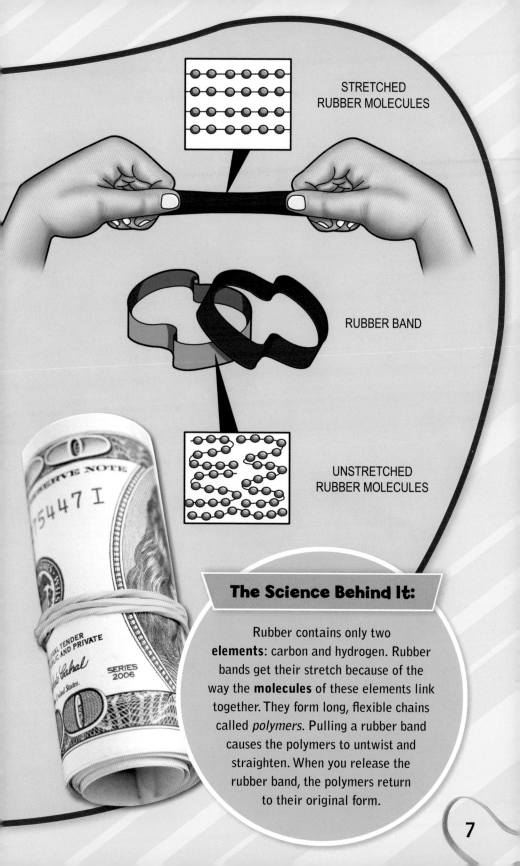

STRETCHED
RUBBER MOLECULES

RUBBER BAND

UNSTRETCHED
RUBBER MOLECULES

The Science Behind It:

Rubber contains only two **elements**: carbon and hydrogen. Rubber bands get their stretch because of the way the **molecules** of these elements link together. They form long, flexible chains called *polymers*. Pulling a rubber band causes the polymers to untwist and straighten. When you release the rubber band, the polymers return to their original form.

Chapter 1

The Science of Stretch

Elastic Magic

No matter how big, fat, or thin, every rubber band stretches the same way. In the 17th century, an English scientist named Robert Hooke used springs to explain how stretchy things stretch. Find out for yourself how Hooke's law works by completing this activity.

▲ Robert Hooke came up with a famous law of elasticity.

Elastic Action

Amazing Stretchable Spoons

What You Will Need:

- two paper clips
- meterstick or ruler
- thin rubber band
- tape
- two tablespoons of the same size and weight

You can use a pen and paper to track your results!

What You Will Do:

1 Fasten a paper clip to the ruler as shown. Bend half of the clip and hang a rubber band through it.

2 Take the second paper clip and attach it to the hanging rubber band. Measure the length of the rubber band when it is not being stretched. Write that number down.

3 Tape one spoon to the hanging paper clip. The weight of the spoon will stretch the rubber band. Record that measurement. Then subtract the length of the rubber band at rest from the length of the stretched rubber band.

4 Tape two spoons to the paper clip. Measure the band again. Subtract the length of the rubber band at rest from the new measurement. What can you conclude?

The Science Behind It:

Two spoons stretch the rubber band longer than one spoon did. The weight of the spoons creates a strain on the rubber band. The stretching changes the length of the rubber band. Hooke's law explains that the strain is proportional to the stretch.

Elastic Challenge

Repeat steps 1 through 4 using other weighty items, such as ink pens.

Change in Temperature

Heat and cold can affect the molecules of most substances. A change in temperature can change how a substance acts and appears. Does heat affect the elasticity of a rubber band? Complete this activity to find out.

Elastic Action — Burning Rubber Bands

What You Will Need:

- medium-sized rubber band
- door with doorknob
- weight such as a hammer (the weight should be heavy enough to stretch the rubber band, but not break it)
- meterstick or ruler
- hair dryer
- glass of ice or a kitchen freezer

You can use a pen and paper to track your results!

What You Will Do:

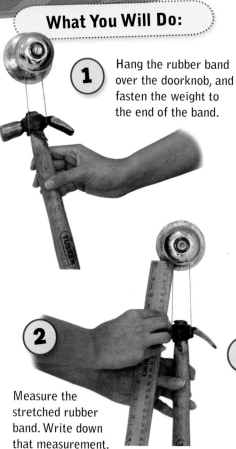

1 Hang the rubber band over the doorknob, and fasten the weight to the end of the band.

2 Measure the stretched rubber band. Write down that measurement.

Direct hot air from the dryer over the rubber band for a few moments. Turn the dryer off and measure the stretched rubber band.

4 Put the same rubber band in a glass of ice or in a freezer for several minutes. Repeat steps 1 and 2. What can you conclude?

The Science Behind It:

When a rubber band expands or contracts, it goes through a process called *entropy*. Entropy is low when molecules are arranged in an ordered fashion. Entropy is high when molecules are arranged in a disordered fashion. When you heat the rubber band, its entropy increases because the molecules start moving faster. When you cool the rubber band, you decrease its entropy by forcing the molecules closer together.

Wacky Elastic

An English chemist named Joseph Priestley coined the word *rubber* in 1770. That is when he discovered that hardened pieces of rubber rubbed out pencil marks.

Spring into Action

Over the centuries, people have used the power of elasticity in creative ways. The catapult is a great example. It was one of the most important weapons used by ancient armies.

Catapults store energy when the arm is pulled back, then quickly release that energy to hurl objects. Ancient catapults fired spears or boulders. But you can hurl marshmallows or Ping-Pong balls using the same principles! Complete this activity to see how a catapult works.

▼ *Real catapults were so big, it took several people to operate them!*

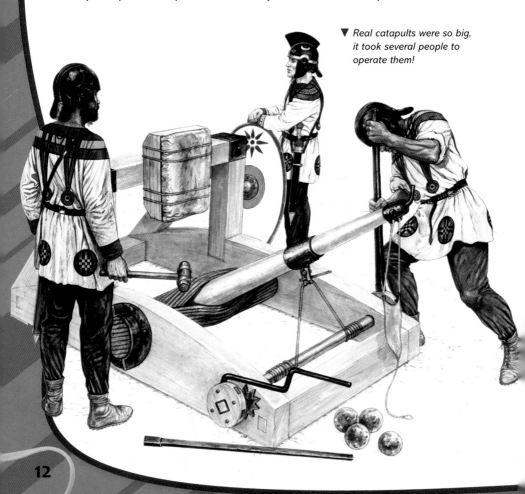

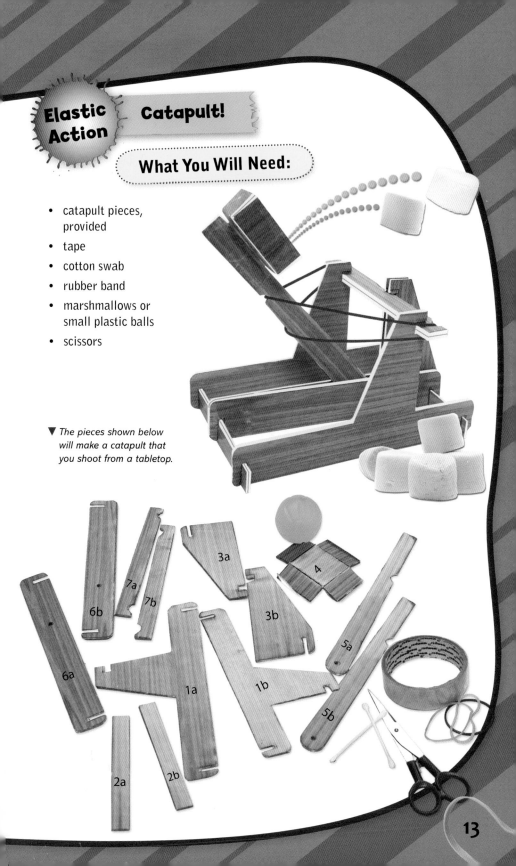

Elastic Action

Catapult!

What You Will Need:

- catapult pieces, provided
- tape
- cotton swab
- rubber band
- marshmallows or small plastic balls
- scissors

▼ The pieces shown below will make a catapult that you shoot from a tabletop.

What You Will Do:

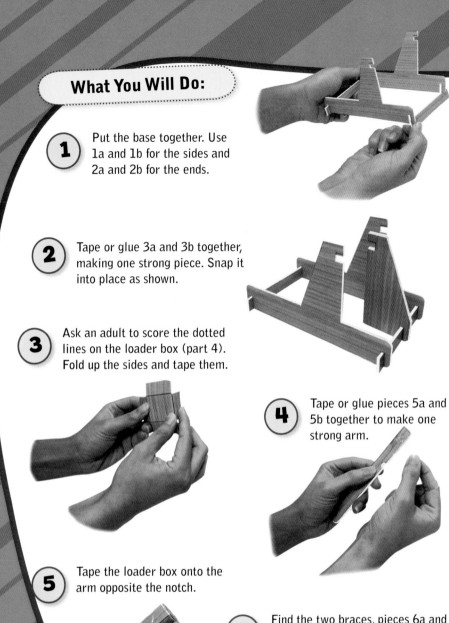

1 Put the base together. Use 1a and 1b for the sides and 2a and 2b for the ends.

2 Tape or glue 3a and 3b together, making one strong piece. Snap it into place as shown.

3 Ask an adult to score the dotted lines on the loader box (part 4). Fold up the sides and tape them.

4 Tape or glue pieces 5a and 5b together to make one strong arm.

5 Tape the loader box onto the arm opposite the notch.

6 Find the two braces, pieces 6a and 6b. Cut a short section from the center of the cotton swab. Use it to attach a brace to each side of the arm by sliding the cut swab through the hole in each piece.

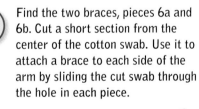

7 Place the arm and braces on the base, as shown. The braces will go on each side of the standing triangular piece. Use tape to reinforce it all.

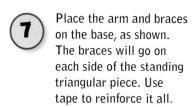

8 Tape or glue 7a and 7b together to make one strong crosspiece. Slide it into the three sail-shaped pieces, as shown. The rounded notches should face away from the arm.

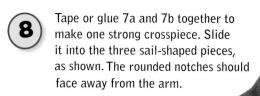

9 Hook the rubber band around the two sides of the crosspiece and in the notch at the back of the arm. Load the box, pull the arm back, and let go!

The Science Behind It:

When you lower the arm, the rubber band stretches and begins storing **potential energy.** When you release the arm, the potential energy becomes **kinetic energy**, which sends the ammunition flying.

Elastic Challenge

Have a marshmallow launching competition outside or in a large room. Pick a set point on the ground or floor from which to launch your marshmallows. Whose go the farthest?

! Shoot away from people or breakables.

15

Crossbow Science

Like the catapult, the crossbow converts potential energy into kinetic energy. Both a catapult and a crossbow use laws of motion, too.

The scientist Isaac Newton wrote the laws of motion in the 1600s. To test how well his ideas work, you can build a simple crossbow.

◄ *Early crossbow strings were made from things like linen or animal tissue.*

Elastic Action

Flying Objects

What You Will Need:

- two rulers or thin pieces of wood about 1 foot (30.5 centimeters) long
- thick tape
- one large rubber band
- Ping-Pong ball

1 Use the rulers to form a "t" as shown. Secure with tape.

3 Look for the loop that is below the "t" bar. Pull it over the top of the "t."

2 Slip the rubber band around the bottom of the "t" and roll it up to where the rulers cross. Pull the band over the top of the "t."

4 Go outside. Pull the top loop back and load the band with the ball. Release the band and ball!

! Shoot away from people or breakables.

The Science Behind It:

Newton's first law of motion says, in part, than *an object in motion tends to remain in motion unless another force acts on it.* The ball wants to keep flying because of **inertia**. The air slows the ball down.

Wacky Elastic

Leo Clouser holds the world's record for the longest rubber band shot. The band flew 99 feet (30.18 meters) on June 18, 1999.

Chapter 3

The Science of Force

Elastic on the Move!

You kick a soccer ball into a goal. You peddle a bike. You run down the street. What do all these activities have in common? There is some sort of *motion* involved. But what causes an object to stop or start moving, or change direction? The answer: force.

Force is a push or pull. Let's see how force behaves by building a rubber band motor.

Elastic Action

Build a Rubber Band Motor

What You Will Need:

- empty spool of thread
- long rubber band that reaches through the spool
- paper clip
- tape
- small metal washer
- cotton swab

What You Will Do:

1 Push the rubber band through the spool. Make sure the band sticks out at both ends. Then insert a small paper clip through one of the loops.

2 Tape the paper clip and the end of the rubber band to the spool.

3 Slide the other end of the rubber band through the washer. Put the tip of a cotton swab through the loop of the rubber band and begin winding.

4 Place the spool on a flat surface. Release your grip on the spool and cotton swab. What happens?

The Science Behind It:

The force generated by the coiled rubber band causes the spool to move.

Elastic Challenge

Measure how far your motor travels. Now, play with your design. You can use a different size spool or a longer or smaller rubber band. Compare each of your designs to see which one works the best.

19

Rubber Meets the Road

Scientists often describe forces by how strong the forces are. Forces can also be described by how they act. Forces can be balanced or unbalanced.

Think of two dogs pulling on a rope with equal strength. That is an example of forces in balance. An object cannot move when forces are balanced. An unbalanced force will cause an object to move or change direction. Try this to see!

▲ If the rope does not move, the force is balanced.

Elastic Action

Race a Rubber Band Roadster

What You Will Need:

- toy car with axles exposed and wheels that turn
- rubber band
- masking tape
- writing tool

You can use a measuring tape, pen, and paper to track your results!

What You Will Do:

1 Take a small piece of masking tape and place it on the floor. Write "Start" on the tape.

2 Tie one end of the rubber band to the front axle with a knot.

3 Stretch the rubber band and wrap it twice around the back axle. Hold the tires tight so they do not yet spin.

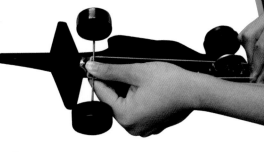

4 Place the front wheels on the starting line. Release the back wheels. How far does the car go?

The Science Behind It:

One force is the push created by the unwinding rubber band. The other is **friction**, which goes in the opposite direction. The push overcomes the friction, and the car moves forward.

Push created by unwinding rubber band

friction working against the push

Elastic Challenge

Repeat the steps, winding the band four times and then eight times. Record your findings. What can you conclude?

Chapter 4

The Science of Flight

High-Flying Elastic

Four forces: *weight, lift, drag,* and *thrust* make flight possible. Weight is caused by **gravity**, which pulls everything down toward Earth. Lift is the force that lifts the wings as air moves over the wings. Drag is the force produced as the plane cuts through air. Drag works against a plane's forward motion. Thrust is the forward force produced by the engine. Thrust overcomes drag. See how by building this air machine.

Elastic Action

Power Rubber Band Planes

What You Will Need:

- airplane parts, provided
- tape (optional)
- slingshot, provided
- rubber band
- paper clips (optional)
- scissors

▼ *Orville and Wilbur Wright made the first motorized plane in 1903.*

What You Will Do:

1 Match the parts for both planes by color. Place the large wings in the front slots. Put the tails in the back slots.

2 Put the two slingshots together, making one thick one. Reinforce the slingshot and planes with tape. Then make one cut in the rubber band. Thread each end into the holes as shown and knot the ends.

3 Place the middle of the rubber band on the notch at the bottom of the plane, as shown.

4 Pull back and release the plane. How far does it go?

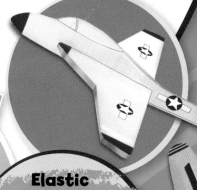

The Science Behind It:

The air moves across the top of the wing faster than it moves below the wing. As a result, there is less air pressure on top of the wing than below. That creates lift, which helps the plane fly. This is known as the Bernoulli effect.

Elastic Challenge

Try placing a paper clip on the nose of your plane. Does that help it fly? Try two clips.

23

Turning Skyward

Twack…twack…twack… twack… A helicopter moves skyward, making that special whirlybird sound. Like an airplane, a helicopter can fly. But it does not fly the very same way. While the **aerodynamic** principles are the same, airplanes only fly forward. Helicopters can go up, down, and even hover in midair. Build this simple helicopter to see how it flies.

▲ The horizontal blades of a helicopter are called rotors.

Elastic Action

Whip Up a Whirlybird

What You Will Need:

- sheet of typing or construction paper
- glue
- thin rubber band

What You Will Do:

1 Cut the paper into two rectangles measuring about 3 inches x 4 inches (7.6 cm x 10 cm). Roll them into two tight cylinders.

2 Glue the edges of each cylinder. Wait for the glue to dry. Bend the tops of the cylinders.

3 Twist the rubber band around the middle of the cylinders.

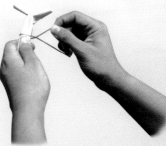

4 While you hold one cylinder in place, twist the other one as tightly as you can. Then let go. What happens?

The Science Behind It:

The rubber band provides the energy that causes the whirlybird's "rotors" to spin. The spinning rotors slice the air, producing the lift the whirlybird needs to fly.

Wacky Elastic

The longest rubber band chain measured 5.19 feet (1.58 m). It was created by Andreas Møller Jensen in Denmark on November 13, 2008.

Elastic Challenge

Use different size rubber bands to see which provides the most power to your homemade helicopter.

Chapter 5

The Science of Sound

The Rubber "Band"

A sound can be as loud as a freight train or as quiet as a whisper. Sounds are produced when objects, such as your vocal cords, vibrate in a **medium**, such as air or water. Those vibrations travel as sound waves.

When the waves reach your ear, they move your eardrum. Your ear then sends a signal to your brain that allows you to hear sounds. If sound waves occur in regular patterns, you hear music. Find out how by building this rubber band guitar.

Elastic Action

String a Rubber Band Guitar

What You Will Need:

- empty rectangular tissue box
- rubber bands of various sizes
- paper, glitter, crayons, stickers
- meterstick or ruler
- tape

What You Will Do:

1 Use paper, glitter, crayons, or stickers to decorate the outside of the box.

3 Tape the meterstick or ruler to the back of the box as shown.

2 Carefully stretch several rubber bands around the opening of the box. Some should be thick; others should be thin.

4 Pluck and strum the rubber band "strings" of the guitar. What do you hear as you pluck the different strings?

The Science Behind It:

Why does each rubber band sound different? The different widths of the bands create different widths of sound waves. **Wavelength** is the distance from the high point of one wave to the next. The shorter the wavelength, the higher the sound!

Wacky Elastic

At sea level, sound travels 700 miles (1,126.54 kilometers) per hour!

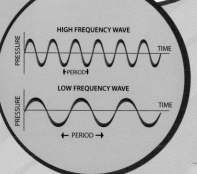

HIGH FREQUENCY WAVE

PRESSURE

TIME

|←PERIOD→|

LOW FREQUENCY WAVE

PRESSURE

TIME

← PERIOD →

Aeolian Sounds

You're home alone. It's dark outside. The wind is howling. Suddenly, you hear strange sounds. Is your house haunted? Not to worry. It's just the electrical lines on a telephone pole whistling.

When the wind blows just right, the power lines make Aeolian sounds. To find out more about these strange noises, complete this activity with an adult.

◄ *When wind passes a fixed object, such as wires, it makes a humming sound.*

Elastic Action

Build an Aeolian Harp

What You Will Need:

- two pieces of wood, 1 foot (0.30 m) long
- two pieces of wood 2 feet (0.61 m) long
- tacks
- tape

- rubber bands of varying sizes and thicknesses
- piece of string about 1 foot (0.30 m) long

An old frame can be substituted for the wood pieces.

What You Will Do:

1 Put the wood together to form a rectangle. Tape the corners, inside and out.

2 Cut a rubber band to make a strip. Tack each end of the strip to the short sides of the box as shown.

3 Repeat with the other rubber bands.

4 Tie the string to the top of the harp. Take it outside and hang it on a tree. Listen carefully. What happens when the wind blows?

The Science Behind It:

When a person walks through a stream of water, the water spins in patterns known as vortices. Air behaves much the same way. When twisting winds pass across rubber bands, the winds make vortices called the von Karman vortex street, and the harp makes sounds.

Wacky Elastic

Every year more than 30 million pounds (13.6 million kg) of rubber bands are sold in the United States.

Elastic Challenge

Loop four rubber bands of the same size into a chain. Hook six paper clips at the chain's bottom. Spin the chain around until it makes Aeolian sounds.

Chapter 6

The Science of Simple Machines

Crazy Elastic

Rube Goldberg was a famous cartoonist with a degree in engineering. He often drew funny cartoons in which complex machines performed silly tasks. Go to www.rubegoldberg.com and look at some of his drawings.

Just for fun, many people have built real machines that look like a Rube Goldberg drawing. Now it's your turn!

Elastic Action

Wacky Works

Try your hand at making a Rube Goldberg machine. It can do anything you want it to do. Should it crack eggs? Pop a balloon? Water a plant? Feed your hamster?

What You Will Need:

- Rubber bands and whatever else you can find around your house!

◄ Rube Goldberg once said that people just seemed to like his "crazy things."

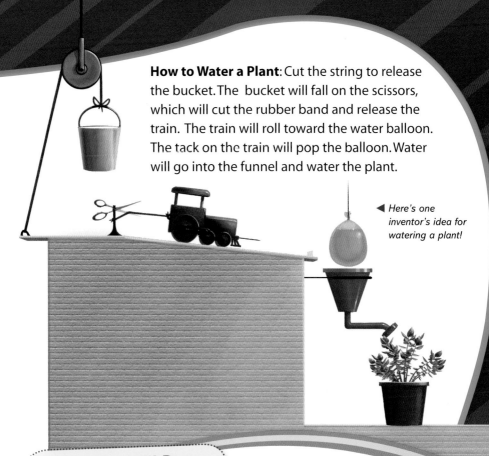

How to Water a Plant: Cut the string to release the bucket. The bucket will fall on the scissors, which will cut the rubber band and release the train. The train will roll toward the water balloon. The tack on the train will pop the balloon. Water will go into the funnel and water the plant.

◀ *Here's one inventor's idea for watering a plant!*

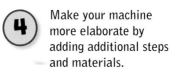

What You Will Do:

1 Brainstorm with friends how your machine could work. Look at illustrations of Rube Goldberg machines for ideas.

2 Sketch out what your machine should look like, designing it in no fewer than 10 steps.

3 Test the machine. Replace parts or steps as needed. Use additional materials if needed. Don't become discouraged if your machine doesn't work right away.

4 Make your machine more elaborate by adding additional steps and materials.

The Science Behind It:

Goldberg machines use energy, gravity, motion, and other forces to complete small jobs. What is the science behind your machine? Explain it.

Glossary

aerodynamic   designed to work well with air flow

elements   the basic substances on Earth, each made of one kind of atom only

friction   force that works against motion when one object rubs another one

gravity   force of attraction between two objects, especially Earth and things on Earth

inertia   the tendency of an object at rest to stay at rest and an object in motion to stay in motion

kinetic energy   energy or power an object has because of its motion

medium   the surrounding environment, such as water or air

molecules   groups of two or more atoms

potential energy   energy or power that is stored in an object

synthetic   human-made; prepared or made artificially

vulcanization   treating rubber a certain way to harden it or to make it more elastic

wavelength   distance from one wave top to another in waves of light, heat, or sound